Look here!

Sally Hewitt

QEB Publishing, Inc.

Library of Congress Control Number:
2005921171

ISBN 1-59566-087-9

Written by Sally Hewitt
Series Consultant Sally Morgan

Project Editor Honor Head
Series Designer Zeta Jones
Photographer Michael Wicks
Picture Researcher Nic Dean

Publisher Steve Evans
Creative Director Louise Morley
Editorial Manager Jean Coppendale

Printed and bound in China

The words in bold
like this are
explained in the
Glossary on page 22.

Contents

See this!

You have five senses that give you all kinds of information about what is going on around you.

The five senses are sight, touch, taste, smell, and hearing. This book is about sight.

Your sense of sight helps you see colors and shapes around you and things that move.

4

Look around you.
What can you see?
What is moving?

▲ Your sight helps you
cross the road safely.

**What colors can
you see? What
colors do you
like to wear?**

▶ When you go
shopping, you
look for things
you like.

5

How you see

Eyes are the part of your body that you see with.

▶ When your eyes are shut, **light** can't get in and you can't see.

The colored circle in your eye is the **iris**.

The black circle in the iris is called the **pupil**. Pupils are holes that let light into your eyes.

iris

pupil

When it is dark, your pupils open to let in light. Your pupils get smaller when it is very bright to stop too much light hurting your eyes.

To see your pupils change size, close your eyes for a minute then open them and look in a mirror. Your pupils look big.

Look out of the window in daylight, then look in a mirror. Your pupils should look smaller!

Look and learn

You can learn all kinds of things when you look carefully.

Look at these children. Can you tell if they are happy or sad?
Can you tell where they are going?

What else can you tell about them just by looking?

Your eyes send messages to your brain about what you see.

Look carefully at these pictures, then cover them up. What can you remember?

ball

plate

flower

rubber duck

How many things are there?
What color is the ball?
What color is the flower?
What else can you remember?

Two eyes

You have two eyes in the front of your head. The **eyeballs** in your eyes move together. They can move up and down, and left and right.

◀ You have to turn your head around to see what is going on behind you.

▶ A chameleon can look up with one eye and down with the other eye at the same time!

Your two eyes help you to tell how far away something is. It is harder to tell with one eye shut.

- Hold your arms out in front of you.
- Put a top on a pen.
- Now try and put the top on the pen with one eye shut.

How easy is it with one eye shut?

How your eyes work

When you look at something, a picture of it is made on the back of your eyes. This picture is upside down!

Lens

Pupil

Light goes in here

Iris

◀ Your brain turns the picture around and you see it the right way up.

Your eyes can see colors clearly in bright light.

What colors can you see in this picture?

In the dark, most colors look gray.

▶ In the dark, you see the shapes of this picture, but the colors could look gray.

Bigger and smaller

Lenses are curved pieces of glass or plastic. They make things look bigger, smaller, nearer, or farther away.

Lenses in a telescope make things look closer.

◀ A planet looks like a dot in the night sky. A telescope makes it bigger.

14

A **magnifying glass** makes things look bigger. The lens is curved and thicker in the middle.

◀ You can see the pattern of your fingerprint under a magnifying glass lens.

Activity

These are objects that have been magnified. Can you tell what they are?

▶ This is a juicy fruit.

◀ You might use this for your hair.

Wearing glasses

The lenses used in glasses help people see things more clearly.

◀ Long-sighted people need glasses to help them read and see things close up.

▶ Short-sighted people need glasses to see things in the distance.

16

◀ Contact lenses
work in the same
way as glasses,
but the lens is
put straight onto
the eye.

Sunglasses have dark
lenses. These lenses
help protect your
eyes in bright
sunlight.

17

Being blind

People who are blind learn to use other senses to give them information.

The sound of someone's voice tells them how that person is feeling.

◀ Blind children use their sense of touch to learn.

▶ Blind children learn to read by feeling raised dots called Braille.

Blind people can find things if they are always kept in the same place.

Why should a room be kept clean for someone who can't see?

▸ This tidy bedroom belongs to someone who can't see. Toys left lying on the floor could be dangerous.

Trick your eyes

Your eyes can be tricked into seeing things that aren't really there.

◀ Look at this picture. Do you see a rabbit or a duck? Or both?

Optical illusions are pictures that look like one thing, but could be another, like the picture on this page.

A movie looks like one long, moving picture, but it is lots of still pictures shown one after another very fast.

Activity

Make your own moving picture!

- Draw 5 pictures like these:

- Put the pages in order like this, and flick them quickly to see the figure run.

Glossary

Eyeballs

Your eyes are shaped like small, round balls. You can see only the front part of your eyeballs.

Iris

The colored part of your eye is called the iris. People have different colored irises such as green, blue, and brown.

Lens

The lens in your eye helps you to see things. Lenses in glasses or binoculars make things look bigger or smaller.

Light

Light comes from the sun, or lightbulbs, or fire. Your pupils get larger or smaller to let in, or keep out, light.

Magnifying glass

A magnifying glass has a curved glass or plastic lens. It makes things look bigger.

Pupil

The black circle in your eye is called the pupil. Your pupils are holes which open and close to let in light or keep out light.

Index

Parents' and teachers' notes

- Divide the class into pairs. Ask the children to identify the pupils and irises in each others' eyes. Guess which is the most common eye color in the class. Make a block graph recording the children's eye colors and compare the result with the children's guesses.

- Play games that involve looking carefully. Show the children a picture, then take it away and ask them questions about it. What have they remembered? *I-Spy* and *Memory* are good games for looking and remembering.

- Collect things that the children can discuss. For example, a page from a children's clothes catalog, famous paintings, flowers, or pieces of material. Ask the children to describe them. Talk about what they like or dislike about the look of them, such as the color or the shape.

- Talk about protecting your eyes. Never look directly at the sun. Sunglasses help protect your eyes from bright sunlight. Goggles help protect your eyes in a swimming pool.

- Look at pictures of animals and talk about their eyes. Are they on the front or sides of their heads? Are their eyes big or small? Do the animals have to see at night or underwater? Do they use their eyes for hunting?

- Explain that we see things when light from them goes into our eyes. Try looking at a bunch of flowers in bright light, in shadow, and then in a dark room. Talk about how the amount of light changes what you can see.